Waking to the Dream

Heidi Elaine Hermanson

D1607734

STEPHEN F. AUSTIN STATE UNIVERSITY PRESS

Stephen F. Austin State Univeristy Press
PO Box 6100, SFA Station
Nacogdoches, TX 75962
sfapress@sfasu.edu
936-468-1078

For information about special discounts for bulk purchases,
please contact Texas A&M University Press Consortium
tamupress.com
800.826.8911

ISBN: 978-1-62288-213-7
Cover and book design by Sarah Denise Johnson
Cover image: Heidi Elaine Hermanson
Page 59, section 3, "Man Eating Yogurt" by Jane Kenyon

For my family
My mentors
My poets and my friends
...and for all the roads in the world

Contents

Waking to the Dream

The moon: beautifully luminous. I want to stay up all night and share a creamsicle sundae with her — one dish, two spoons.

After Larry Levis' Motel Room

Shiny on the outside
is more than just a metaphor
for some things. You only need
a few things—
a TV with cable, a swimming pool,
a liquor store you can walk to.
My six pack
filled, I gaze out the window
watching the city lights. If
I were still smoking I would
have dramatically stubbed
the cig out by now.
I like being anonymous
in a town whose name
I can't pronounce. I like
leaving my towels around
for someone else to pick up. The
stamp-sized motel soap
freshens the air. Cools it.
I lie back—
the last time I did this
I was young and naïve
thinking at that time
that everything would last
forever. Nothing lasts
any longer than
a match struck and then blown out,
a puff of smoke,
a crush, a stub out,
holding back the darkness.

The Poet at Seventeen

It's funny what you remember: the green couch,
the newspapers strewn everywhere. I could not pick them
up fast enough; they would multiply.
Submerged in her Beefeater martini,
immersed in the telly, my mother didn't bother
too much with too much of anything.
The paper's headlines, "Watergate Scandal."
"Skylab launched into space."
"Egypt and Israel sign cease-fire agreement."
The local paper, in end-of-the-world, 150-point type read,
"WE ARE FROZEN."
I thought that winter would go on forever,
and it seemed to. Outside the snow fell
and the temperature kept dropping.
There was no cease-fire here: 4710 Huntington, raised ranch-style
house on a dead end in front of a farmer's pasture,
and beyond that, a cemetery, Forest Lawn,
neither forest nor lawn. Always the train call,
insistent and lonely. Rushing ahead
to the lush spring, I took the inside
to the outside, wandered the farmer's
fields, the cemetery at night, fingered the pain delicately
like a tongue on a sore tooth. Hoping some man
would come along, put me
in one of those reserved plots.
I honed my sorrow, my marrow, hardened
myself for the hardness to come. I lay
flat on my stomach, groundless, guileless,
carefully copied "Casey's Coast to Coast" Top 40
every week into my spiral notebook.
Sunday night, and the music was my religion.
As Casey mixed the wax, I slid slowly,
waiting for all the answers

that would ever come. That would never come.
He always finished the top 40 with,
"Keep your feet on the ground,
and keep reaching for the stars."
I pined while he opined, laid
stars open like a sheet,
casually surveyed the wreckage.
Do you know that the music
was all that ever kept me from floating
out the window into the tombs beyond,
a bright butterfly, wings slowly being crushed?

Emotions embalmed,
I searched relentlessly for that exit door,
nearly went through a time or two.
I was perilous, in critical condition. I was seventeen.
Then, my Mom's Mensa parties,
click of ice and drunken laughter
invaded my blue room. The occasional
quizzical look if I happened to wander
out into the festivities. Her friend Jim
would try to talk to me, back me into a corner.
Picasso, Matisse, he knew all of it.
Back in those years,
before Jim slashed up his paintings
with a knife, then turned it on
himself. Artfully. See, even Jim
didn't have all the answers. He once told me I should listen
to jazz, that it would change me, change my life
but all he was really trying
to do was get me alone.
Him and me and Sonny Rollins,
years later, lying in bed, flushed and radiant, insistent train call,
a comforting old friend. I forgave the past,
leaned in to kiss my future hello.

Interval

Why stay awake skipping sacred stones
across pools of thought,
splashing in strutting light?
Egg-yolk sun skimming
like water at twilight;
siphoning time (circa forever),
and what's absurd.
Brashness foisted reluctantly
resonates, soused, lousy with joy.
Sic Transit Gloria.
Sidewalk sweeps pollen flecks:
the moist breath of summer
saunters, laggard.
Planes, mistaken for fireflies, lurch;
fireflies mistaken for stars, see-saw,
sashay askew. Intricate weavings, interlocked.
True or true-shaped.
Audacious.

It was the spring before we moved, again

It was the summer after you left
I smoked extra cigarettes,
drew my eyes
toward bright clouds crammed
and sharp blades of grass
as if that would matter
as if one more detail of beauty would be
      somehow significant
to my crooked little crock pot heart
my dust rag heart
dusting up every hurt and sorrow ever known to man,
crumpling
I was a desert, soaking my hurts
in an amber pool
and no snorkel
I was a paddle, splashing wildly
as if that would have made any difference
to you
to anyone
I gasped for breath
taking in all the potential beauty
before going under.

"First they walk on your feet…"

"…then they walk on your heart"
my mother-in-law intones, but this one only makes my
heart softer and more tender – maybe in preparation for her
to walk on it.
Her ice blue eyes fix themselves intently on me
as if to memorize each wrinkle, each one a road map.
Her smile transcends all time.
The future is not promised,
but she is a seal and a testament to it,
a mile marker that flicks out
quick as a lit cigarette burning down to the very end.
I hold my niece, think of her future,
she's as tart as an unripe pear.
Her skin is as soft as the inside of my heart.
Her specialty: softening hearts.
Time races on. Each move, our hands, our eyes,
describes a burden,
the baggage we carry.
We drag it through snow,
leaving marks on the ground, scars.

Letter to My Adventist Grandparents, Who Were Once Missionaries

Dear Abuelitos,
The sunset here wears an orange hat with blood-red streaks.
Do you feel slightly guilty about enjoying it?
Or does it remind you
to preach about the Sangre de Cristo

and think about the life after this life.
You gifted me with offerings from
your cold country,
and that coldness
came out in your demeanor:
stern faces, lips pursed over
dry creek beds of wrinkles.
Grandparents, enlightening the heathens
of their eternal salvation on the darkest continent,
you of everyone know that life is a gamble,
throw out the bones and see what comes up.
Even a sweet sugar skull, sparkly and gritty,
would be forbidden in your religion.
The skull is grinning
because he knows how the story ends.
But he's the only one, and he's not telling.
Dear Abuelitos, I would like to see you again,
gently hold your wrinkled hands in mine.
I also know that you have never
stopped loving me. Your love
is as permanent as a name carved in stone.
You taught me so many times by example,
without saying a word.
My bones are picked clean of contention.
I break like a matchstick.
Grandpa, play a ferocious hambone rhythm in the sky.

Don't stop there.
Let you and Grandma waltz raucously
for the first time, laughing wildly.
Slurp sugar skulls.
Thank you for your prayers for me.
I will break open the ofrenda of my heart,
light a candle for you. Life is but a dream,
and a dream yet another life.
Con todo mi amor.

Yearn

As the evening news makes clear, the starving and the besieged maintain the current standard of beauty without effort. —Jane Kenyon, Fat

You wear your scrawn like a badge of honor. You feed on your self-esteem and you are devoured. You turn to your also-thin friends for validation, but your slip of a girlfriends are not the apple-pie kind type. The fate is the fact you keep remembering, one after the other. You suck in your own self-loathing, hungry for applause. There are so many bones to pick apart. Don't cut yourself open.

At the Downtown Y

I want to do the weight machine barefoot
in this cavernous clink
echoing with the grunts
of baboons and gorillas.
Throw those blocks in the air
and watch them make impact.
Plant flowers in the hair
of the gorillas and silverbacks pumping iron
in a never ending circle of metal and sweat.
There's one lone wolf
you just know would put you on the six o clock news
faster than you could say Stop
but
in my world, everyone is awesome.
All the women look like Jennifer Flashdance
and all the men are a variation of Bob Birdsong on toast.
Kellie shows up with an aquamarine fit suit
and what actually looks like...a whip?
She megawatts that "you know what would be FUN?" grin.
The men fall helplessly to their feet, unbound.
As for Wolfie, He's just another whiff of smoke
to be blown out.

At Patrick's Market

I ran into my ex in the supermarket—
That in itself was a cliché of sorts
I hadn't seen him since I was 18 years old,
I am pleased to report he looks disheveled and beat up
His eyes still the color of coal, though, and
his skin curry-colored.
I was trying to get my debit card to work,
a feat that apparently involved three clerks and two managers
and the plastic bag trick
(which sounds like a weird sex thing
but isn't).
We all gave up after about eight minutes
and I pulled my debt card out,
Well, I thought I was saving time by stopping here...
Good things are worth waiting for, but
some things aren't worth the effort you exert
in calories or chocolate.

The Red Kite and the Lemonade Stand

You might say I stopped at the post office on a whim.
The first thing I pulled out of the mail box was a card
from Charlene which had a story
about red kites in winter on it. This
pleased me immensely. It also turned
out to be a portent, for I next took out
a red card that said, "Package too large
for your mailbox. Please collect
around the corner." I rang and rang
and no one answered. I crossed
the boundary waters to the mail clerks' area,
two of them. Two customers also, one having a hard
time deciding between options,
one with four packages inquiring
as to the clerk's personal history
for the last six years. Finally, a woman
in front of me on a cell,
directly by the sign that said, "Please
finish your conversations *before*
approaching the counter."
In the time
I could have had six children
and sent them to college
I made it to the counter. A friendly
stocky man with a gray beard and a nametag
that read JASON greeted me kindly,
and, like a shaman, said he'd meet me back
on the other side. After some crashing
and scraping he appeared from behind the door
with a grocery cart containing a very large box.
It was Francesca's box! Huzzah! He looked uncertainly at me.
"You have someone to *help* you
with this?" he asked. "Can you leave

it in the cart and I'll bring the cart back?"
I asked him. He nodded.
I realized when I got to my car

the box wasn't fitting
in the Hyundai, so I did what any mad-
man would do, I opened
the car door, pulled the seat
forward, pulled the cart closer, opened
the box and began tossing
literary journals of all stripes
in the back seat,
until the box was a manageable
weight. Wait. Then threw
the box, still half-filled
with lemons
in the front passenger seat.
Goddess, lemons!
I can sell lemonade out of my car.
I can be a moving lemonade stand.
I can be an old-fashioned
Bookmobile and sell lemonade
and lemon margaritas
and fancy lemon drinks
and salads with lemons out of my car.
I can slice lemons, and more lemons
arrange them like so many suns
on an atypically warm Nebraska day
in February.

At the Calmar Guesthouse

It was just like staying
at my grandmother's house:
Her wrinkled face beamed
to see me. She put me
in a star-filled room
gleaming with dark mahogany.
It was redolent with lavender,
trimmed with old lace curtains
flitting in the breeze
from the half-cracked windows.
Outside, the moon peeped in.
The nightstand was choked
with Precious Moments.
On one wall: pictures of Jesus as
    The good Shepherd, serious, diligent;
    Himself, in casual robe and sandals,
    stared back at me. The wallpaper—
    a curious, twisted rose pattern.

"This is usually the room the newlyweds
stay in. You can be married to Jesus tonight."
A pause. "Or one of the angels."
Exuberant newlyweds had taken it
out of the bed, which resembled
the Sandhills in shape. I tossed and turned,
twisted the plaid-patterned sheets
as the house settled, and settled,
and all night long the wind sang Mary,
and Jesus never did show up, homemade wine
in one hand, box of Trojans
in the other (what would Jesus do?)
It was just as well—he'd have complained
about the bed, and the wind, and his mother,
hovering above.

The Zen Monk Contemplates His Life Choices

I should be full of peace and compassion
sitting on this hill that encompasses the world.
The scent of lilac wafts over me
from a nearby garden,
the veil of uncertainty.
The tolling of a nearby bell
calls me to prayer.
I run my hands over my smooth
brown prayer beads,
hear the sound of rattles,
so like bones.
This is and shall be my life,
a part of my life
like the orange that I am draped in.
Back to the hill. The head priest
has made it snow,
and is gleefully tobogganing
downward.
I blow away with the sand mandala.

The Carrying Over

This is a ferry to another life,
beams stuck on high, gaze
unwavering towards the future.

What seems like a dilapidated wreck
of rotten planks is bejeweled inside,
encrusted with glory,
an open letter to the ocean.

There are no leather-clad,
whip-brandishing
personal trainers here,
just softly-rounded women
who resemble your dear, blue-
haired grandmother long gone.
They wear fragrant white face powder
and clunky jewelry. They cluck
softly, smile knowingly,
and nod approvingly
at the inanest of your remarks.

It is not a matter of boarding
or not boarding. The pull is strong,
the rope the sail rides on, rippling.
The launch is now.

See how the ocean clears
a path before you! The lime and lapis
sea-foam dream sparkles as you ride
out the storm. You are safe
below where it's dark.

There is no fear for time,
for the clocks have long since
been thrown overboard,
along with your checkbook,
spare glasses, and mortgage.

Days Lost

In spite of the allergies
I tested negative for,
the heat, the humidity,
the mosquitoes,
in spite of the lost ones,
the lost jewelery,
the lost poetry,
the children that were
in my arms one day and walking out the door next—

In spite of muddy shoes
on my heart's just waxed-floor
(my garbage can heart, you walked away
like a grinning trash man with a pit-bull smile)
In spite of heart aches, body aches
that feel like jays screaming...

In spite of cold stares, my darling,
your face betrays the reluctant wonderment
of the world as you sashay
through August heat
with the ease of water-skiing—perfect,
a day with no obligations,
a gazelle in someone else's tomato patch,
a shimmering white veil,
a white mosquito veil
over your small heart.

The Brass Ring

The summer I was 17 I worked
in a bowl factory, wrapping rings:
Toilet bowls, wax rings. Floyd the owner
liked to park his rusty baby blue Seville
right by the front door. His plates read:
BOL WAX. I walked around the Cadillac,
three steps down into pale light,
where musty damp mixed with smoke.
Every day I passed a yellowed calendar,
each completed day X'd off;
a life sentence to be endured. Some lifers
had grim pale pinched faces that looked
as if they had never seen daylight.
In sneakers and shorts we stood for hours,
carefully swathing the life-save shapes
in opaque plastic, unpretentious piss color.
This was after you'd left.
But I stood brave, didn't look for a life preserver,
though I wavered on both feet, went by feel,
grief kicking in quickly, kicking me
in the head, the heel.
I nearly tripped on the cracked, damp
concrete floor I stood on, kicking the mustardy sky,
the not-clear paper I was wrapping wax rings in
as they wandered on the production line, tangling
hopelessly, tangoing with the rage that draped me,
Lucy wrangling in the chocolate factory,
only worse, nothing sweet to eat here,
bundling something that would go in someone's toilet.
I had not yet begun to write.
It seemed like the perfect metaphor to me.

Drumming into Good Friday

With nothing but fragile skin and breath,

bury hurt
and resentment
and drum.

Listen. Concentrate on each move,
pay attention to your breathing,
as we sound out the right
rhythms of the universe,
and stars call back to us as we
bleed old secrets out of our skin.

Our hearts will pulse
in time,
our fingers numb—
the full moon glows widely,
peeking in, amused
at us small ones—

Night unfolds its shawl
we all—you and wind and rain—
break wide open
diffusing rhythm and pain.

Sing the ancient sounds
as stars scatter
and we hammer out our life.

Death On the Installment Plan

"It's okay, some people are quick learners
and some aren't," the trainer reassures me.
Evidently I belong in the special
children's school. The boys waiting in line
talk smack about me and finally move on.
I have two degrees
—neither of them are in plastic bags.
Autistic kids often see 60 flickers
per second in fluorescent lights. Bright lights,
no music. Music to shop by
would add another crispy layer
to this inferno cake. The trainer puts a plug
of chew between her remaining teeth, snorts.

Memento Mori—Remember That You Are Mortal

We are transients, our short stint,
nothing more than a twig
that randomly snaps in two, no more significant
than a stain from a wine glass
laid carelessly on yellow parchment.

We dawdle as shadows darken,
gaslight reality,
shrug at time's larceny
as we loiter, gazing off into the distance,
deep in thought, preoccupied.

A lull. Here are the kids,
precious faces, serious, stoic,
darkened eyes staring into the future.
In the background, some books,
some wine—everything you need, really.

The shroud of recollection
is a wistful veil, how time smudges
memory in a soft lens!

Under nocturne, rogue stars revealed,
—all sparkle and crushed glass—
and covered everything,
like a mantel. Even time.

But now our limbs tremble, we surrender and
abandon everything as the minute hand abscond with our bones,
time varnishes our memories in warm sepia tones,
a lens we fall through willy-nilly.
Dazed, we pick a small bouquet of moments,
salvage our few futile remnants,
grudgingly, tearfully remit our
squandered pension.

My new friend confesses and commences to waltzing
nostalgic for age 39.

Bury your fears in these sunflowers,
inhale deeply.
In these precarious hours,
you are radiant, lavish.

Tethered in Arms

Dusk.
Drunk, spent,
clothes, cares a tangled heap, twisted to the wind,
we lie near a tombstone marked
CHAVAS JULY 1, 1884—JULY 10, 1902,

in this covert graveyard off the road,
ground awash with pink prairie roses.

Staring at cloud formations,
I'm wondering about squandering
the moment—although I suspect I already have—

But you're having none of it. None of the gossamer breeze,
the lavish birdcall, the sun. You are practical, not lyrical.
Stroking my hair, you say, "We will go
too someday—does that make you sad?" Honest as piss.

I shrug, as much as one can tethered in arms. After this
particular confluence, I am an imbecile only speaking babble anyway,
a carrier of joy, convoluted, my hallelujahs going sideways.
This gospel, indelible.

Soon will come the season of drawn bones
and cantankerous wind making a dismal carousel of leaves.
Fall's a brittle casualty, trawling for sorrow.

Back to your question though—time's underhanded tactics.
what makes bridal veil, ornamenting
the side of the road, so very beautiful
is the abbreviated sense of time.

But now—blushed sun, endless sky,

clouds illuminated, vibrant and odd,
like clothes, wadded and discarded.

It is just then we notice the portal, the open grave, its hungry mouth
gaping, yearing for a stew of bright bones.

We lie and time lies before us, within us, and to us. Blithely we bluff to the end,
purge the darkness, give death the finger.

Cemetery

A cemetery is a rest stop
in the quietest of cities.
You can stretch your legs, breathe deep,
walk among the hushed,
read the condensed version
of their life.

I've stumbled on those better angels,
mossy, cracked, some missing a hand or a wing,
small faces earnest, as if holding fast,
sworn to secrecy.

No time is squandered better:
drowsing on sun-warmed earth,
staring at stippled shadows
that chase down hours.
That is to say, the sundial is frozen.

Quiet except for the
sibilant syllables
of a wood-bound bird.
The wind, of course, and
each blade of grass
quivering, clouds low and brooding

as you stalk lush moments,
taking every morsel,

you can finally testify,
no—those sleeping below can say,
they have all the time
in the world.

Not Exactly the Love Song of J. Alfred Prufrock

Let us not even go there, you and I,
Where the evening lays down its dreams
like an abandoned cardboard box.
When I follow you
through certain streets
I know peril lurks
but I go anyway
down those cobblestones that reflect
the skies of congealed blood
(those bricks that sang the moonlight)
to the back rooms.
Stop asking me the question
you already know the answer to.

The evening spills out its dreams:
The lush twilight air
so thick you can taste it,
summer air that wraps
around you like a shawl.

You think that there will always be time
For coffee and beer and poetry and laughter
(and yet more revisions),

As long as you remember that
everything can change in a minute.

When we walk the Market at dusk and dawn
and dusk watching the smoke rise
and the tourists who come and go
don't forget to ask yourself
if you dare. When the eyes fix you in a stare,
crush the butt out and move on.

I hope you have the strength
to force the moment to its crisis.
We are all a flicker, and afraid.

Let's have another cup of coffee,
you and me,

and read poetry to each other,
and not be so presumptuous
as to have squeezed the Universe
into a ball.

I believe that once you realize you are a fool
the rest is easy. Back home, I pull out my
Steely Dan album, *Aja,* the one with
"Home at Last," a retelling of
Odysseus. (There's a reason
people call them Mensa rock.) You smile,
confident in your ability
to ward off any sirens.
Eventually we both fall asleep.

Minimum Maintenance

I know the secret of dusty dirt roads:
Pavement ends: fun begins.

Time has me by the throat
a moat of inconsistency and
old-fashioned sepia tones.

This rough rutted, deep-baked road
of cornfields and silk fields

as well as corn, bittersweet, bridal veil,
weeds, and those shredded wheat roll things,
leaving Nebraska in the dust
and I'm making silk purses out of this day

The sky's a perfect purple green.
Milky clouds scuttle before the storm.

It's 3 p.m. languid
on the hottest day of the year,
the drunk afternoon air.

I be like a rusty tractor
stuck in a field next to
a hedge of exquisite flowers. Yellow and white ones.

The noise to signal ratio
is darn near none here. Tiny white blooms
burst out unexpectedly.

The sign reads, **Highway 275.**
That may or may not be true.

The X of the railroad signs,

railing against boredom. X marks the spot.
A train track long in disuse and since forgotten.

Weeds, dust.
The thrill of the bob-o-link trill,
that scoundrel that absconds with my heart.

The thrill of joyriding with no particular
place to go

and likewise "What lies beyond?
I want to know."

The tree branch traces a filigree
design in the sky.

What is it about a deadpan dusty road,
not showing its hand,
that appeals so?

We breathe dust as we drive,
the dust settling like flour.
We come from dust.

This season is not known for its words
but its sounds and smells,
insane cicada love songs
the new-cut grass,
the wind in my hair.

This season, a luscious bucket of joy,
a kid-gloved afternoon.
A still pool

a fine, full, free-fall of blush
and chardonnay.

The end of the trail.
The long and winding road cut short.
My love, the road has
come to a standstill.

The center winds inward
into an ever-expanding
circle into the Universe.

Accepting the things
that can be accepted.

A rest stop for the weary.

Where does the road go when
it has nowhere to go? Where
is the turn in the curve?

What lies beyond is a mystery, dust
tendrilling thorough late light,
sun spreading through the grove,
the dove of evening spreads her wings.

The place where there is no time.

I know the secret of dusty dirt roads.

The Ex at the Art Opening

My dear,
I speak to you now without crying.
In fact this confluence
is much more hilarious
than I could have ever imagined.
Time doesn't heal wounds;
time wounds heels.
I would love you still
comb-over and all,
had you not tried to cover up
so many *other* things—

The Perfect Day Off

I will hand you the simultaneous and sequential scents of grass, soil,
    honeysuckle, and good whiskey.
You can tell me tales from your childhood and I will reassure you that, like all
    bad dreams, they will vanish by morning.
We can discuss the theological implications of the boundary waters of the
    clouds both prior to and after their impending dissipation.
We will analyze both the softness of the summer breeze and the brightness
    of the sun.
We will notate and document cottonwood flier pilots.
We will go a long way back in time.
We will talk about the breath and you will show me the secrets of the breath
    without either irony or innuendo.
Regarding muscle memory, we will be given an opportunity to be healed and
    heal.
Regarding tears, there is ever room for them.
Of winged creatures and their song: They are another love song you have
    yet to learn.
Of the Fibanocci: Aren't you glad God chose not to hold everything for the
    last minute?
Of the cemetery and of those who rest below:
Hush.
Of milkweed.
Of your locks, and of your keys, and of your broken locks.
Of swimming under sorrow and finally breaking above the surface.
There is no jump to the moment, no text,
Only time spread out, a luscious picnic waiting to be devoured bite by bite.
It is better to be brave than safe, better to tear up, to stay quiet and wait.
Steeped in grief, bathed in joy, I will hand you fresh strawberries,
an LP, a sailboat, a placid pond, a map of the universe,
a map of the county, and a map of my body.
What you choose to do with these is up to you.

Colorful

I want to be friends,
hang out. I want to walk
in the wilderness, discuss
deep things, drink
plain brewed coffee with milk.
Go to open mikes, go to concerts.
He says no, pushing
me away, pushing
the sand-colored hair
out of his muddy Missouri River eyes to glare
at me. His expression is set
to default to glare. I know better
and am not intimidated.
He says, "Men and women
can't be friends. Stop it." he says.
I've heard this before,
maybe in a movie. Yes,
that old movie
where they end up kissing
at the top of the
Empire State Building at midnight
on New Year's Eve. Epic.
"I am not a goddamn booby
prize," she quivers, then abruptly
changes her mind. It always confused
me. He throws the rosary I gave him
my direction. I had explained it was a rabbit foot,
a gem, not a door to another life.
I believe in many shades of gray,
maybe not fifty, maybe 600 colors sparkling
through a badly-cut religious artifact.
I prophesy he will be all alone
in his black and white world.

Letter to New York City

Your lips do not remember me
any more than a cloud.
Some would say unaware.
I am not so sure.
I am no more pure
than wind in trees—
or where we stand.
When I asked you, your
silence curled around me,
leaves across a silent pond.

Your words, dumbfounded church bells
exchanging trust for secrets.

Peeling off another layer,
how do you turn away effortlessly?
After you have shown me
your arteries, your city, who can
resist riding the back of night
into the thrust of dawn,
stars breaking open,
stars making a break for it?

The Season

It is the season of glistening fresh roses
and drawn chilled bones,

plump chocolates
and harsh wind.

The heart's a rough rutted road traveled often,
a cracked window letting the winter wind in
scrabbling toward the drawn dawn.

Smeared there, a patchwork quilt

or something that flutters

snow falling into open mouth

and onto roses.

Inside me these days is a piece of night,
another star in a moonless sky.

Perched on the fire escape of my heart.

Jump.

Emergency Instructions

In case of fire, do not break glass.

In case of fire, lean coolly against the wall, cigarette dangling from your lips.

In case of fire, polish your pliers.

In case of fire, practice your plies, gently bouncing on the balls of your feet.

In case of fire, put your lips together and blow.

In case of fire, remember what your mother said about clean underwear.

In case of fire, repeat his name until it becomes gibberish on your tongue.

In case of fire, scream like bloody murder invaded your neighborhood and
you are the only bandages.

In case of fire – start a committee.

In case of fire, have your will and advanced directives ready.

In case of fire, grit your teeth. Pray.

In case of fire, take the steps.

In case of fire, kiss the boy—kiss the boy you've always wanted but never
spoken to.

In case of fire, ignore the icy silence, use up all your favors, cash in all your
chips, go off the edge,

descend from the fire escape—

all drunken, molten goddess and twisted scrap metal.

A Brush with Love

Your body, a controlled substance,
your tongue, a loaded weapon—

If I am facing you in a battle of wits,
I stand not only unarmed, but blind and naked.

My arms are weary
yet you think me strong.

I am a fraction of myself—
No one need know I am a placid lake

flatted against September blue sky.
Love: the tick of the clock,

relentless, predictable, grinding.
The turning key,

keys secure in pocket,
struggling with time.

Does it make any difference to love beauty
when nothing is solid beneath my feet?

Still, everything brings me to this point,
my locked pockets of resentment,

a break in the moment,
a splinter in time,

Unfurl your silence like a tattered flag
The sounds around pay no heed—

your picture, a record of a moment.
Your voice, a recording of a moment long gone.

No, let us sit in the grass and count leaves,
hunker down, curled up cozy

to nap, perhaps to dream,
the alphabet of rain.

Let us play jacks and marbles and tag,
connect the dots,

tongue counting the ways.
Let us pray.

The Lure of Orange

Because you can stay mum, my love, I will show you a secret, here behind the hill. Bring a rope. Bring a bottle of foreboding, a flashlight, a blindfold. Bring a gun. Everything vanishes by tomorrow. There are long shadows in the nearby valley.

Crooked Little Villanelle

So there we were, the holy Trinity
And I was out late, that made it my fault.
You promised that you'd soon dispose of me.

You cursed and spilled your hatred over me
Not in a million years would you get caught
So there we were, the holy Trinity.

Your one-word reason, "Tease," you said with glee,
Slammed face down, petrified, of course I bought
Your promise that you'd soon dispose of me

I sometimes wonder, are you sorry?
Oh, not that fake remorse for getting caught—
So there we were, the holy Trinity.

Sometimes, unbidden, feelings rise in me
When people tell me, this is how I ought
to feel, or "All things happen for a rea-

son." They nod and they expect me to agree.
Well. How would *you* respond? "Why don't you rot
In hell…You and the Holy Trinity."
And I was out late, that made it my fault.

April

In April, the enemy
took up residence in her head,
explaining in a soothing voice
how much better death is than life. He cajoles,
the dirty one that explains
how much cleaner he is than her.

He says if she were good
she would be good, but because she's not,
she's not even memorable.

Come back—come back to where
you were before,
to a room filled with white flowers
open windows
and lush warm breezes.

It is April which means
she is gunning her reinforcements
with the tenderness of old leather:
the ermine-lined sledgehammer.
She knows to crush diamonds every day.
They cut her. She scatters them
to walk in.

Her scaffolding, failing,
a deflated balloon crumpling.

Come back—come back to where
you were before,
to a room filled with white flowers
open windows
and lush warm breezes.

Squandering the Moment

Curtains flit,
sorbet sunrise spills brash blush
on my chenille spread.
All the clocks broken.
We jostle, careen with chaos,
I melt, empty out, petals,
sing silk, heady honey, shimmering jazz phrase at midnight.
Quietly we ignite,
a bouquet of bridal veil and rosemary
spilled by the side of the road.
Introduce me to the inside of your wrists,
the back of your throat,
the one that catches with joy.
Bestow on me your secret.
I can be single celled,
one lush pocket of pleasure. I have faith,
I have faith, your hair a prayer shawl
draped everywhere, I'm reading avidly, greedily,
my Bible, my Koran,
my lips rest on your pages,
all knowledge, good and evil,
the lost cause unlocked
with keys we never knew existed,
unlocking the breastbone,
cracking open the wishbone. Feel free to grant all my wishes.
Out here there are no stars,
no stripes, no patriot laws, out here we
waltz slowly to ancient melody,
play connect the constellations.
Out here there are no lines, no walls, just laughter, deftly enveloping
a bootleg peace accord
bound by skin and breath,
the orchard of your arms,

our personal vineyard. Draw this moment taut into forever,
sink deeper into the swirling eddies,
bliss twining again into bliss.
Who knew you could play a symphony on broken strings?
We dilute, crawl helplessly toward the fluttering light.

To Your Wife

"I am a watercolor. I wash off." —Anne Sexton

Adrift in a corner, you seethe.
I can feel it.
You look at me with
two parallel lines on your brow
as if I would spirit him away
into a classical painting
of a picnic on the grass,
a checkered blanket,
some wine,
and me the main course.
Even Manet knew better.

You frown,
concerned that my light touch on his shoulder
means more than it means.

I will not lie to you. I will not tell you
I never thought about it.
But there are miles between
thoughts and actions.

Look at me. I am neither fragile and ethereal
nor candid and unfettered.

He is not dumb.
He stood beside you, as your mother cried
crystalline drops in the background
of your perfectly orchestrated day
(laughing, awkward, brilliant. Those fetching lines in the corner of his eyes)
and swore before God and everyone
to love you forever.

You must believe he meant it
if you are to survive. He
has buffed you to a fine shine,
your skin glowing, burnished.
Your eyes glow. You're a luscious ripe pear waiting to split open.
You sleep soundly next to him,
his arm curled protectively around you.
As you sleep, I will be thinking
of every way there was,
every piece of fruit touched and eaten—
There is a difference between word and deed,
between longing and having.
He waits for you, smooth and solid.
You are well-tended hothouse orchids and lilies.
I'm a reed in April gales.

To the Words I Forgot

Maybe I was almost asleep
when you presented yourself to me—
Maybe I was doing 50 down a fine dirt road.
Maybe he had just reached out his hand,
tentative, shy
or maybe it was just afterward,
limpid as jellyfish, languid, spent.
Maybe I was down, eyes closed,
feeling the earth spin.
Maybe I was wiping away the last tear,
vowing to cry no more that year.

After the Flood

1. From the 40th story of the Missouri River, we stand transfixed, everything around us pure air. Cloud cover passes through our bodies. Your mouth, sigh-shaped, dovetails, none too close for comfort, your summer stars as if lit. As the water splits, grows wider, we throw off veils. Holding on to the wind like a kite tail, woefully adrift, the breeze, your breath, we set sail for the new land, hope patchworked.

2. I led you to the edge of the levee. Showed you the secrets there, showed you everything I knew. Your silence filled up the void. You stand, poised as if to leap. Deep waters don't run still. Fill me up another time, climb all the way up. Cup my cheeks, hold my hands in your hands. A world within a world. Pearls, chills. Afraid of what we might feel, our emotions funneled, a small stream, facts rushing over us. Memories float by, much debris. Ankle-deep, I wade through.

3. We began with breath, because we know how to breathe, as we did from the beginning, evermore. While we first walked gingerly barefoot over rocks, the water from the river seeped up silently. We lay down then, expectant, innocent.

4. You slip, your hands free, your face indistinct and distorted as if viewed from underwater, each breath another black butterfly. I overflow my banks like a good river. Whirlwinds and eddies. Heavens, the Jordan overflows. We take the miracles for granted. We wash in the river. We splash in the water, our faces smeared with mud, our eyes closed.

5. I hang sheets of rain as they begin to fall—great soft flannel blowing against the dark. They tie me up in knots. For a moment I listen to the wind, breath filling me with life we both loved and scorned, a little thorn pricking us, our drops of blood diluting days.

6. [...]

7. When the fires begin, we exhale gently. The end of the world is no end, just another beginning. Out faces glow from the light. The sky's the color of copper. We are fine metal, glowing. In cracks of light, we see ourselves reflected. We are illuminated, pinks and greens. The forests wash away. The levee of your heart will slowly breach. Those wet messages written in the sand which will wash away. Finding no solid land to stand on, we give ourselves over to water.

My Relationship with God

Interrogation first thing in the morning before coffee.
Hearing only the bass of "Free Bird" over and over through the neighbor's wall.
The roller coaster ride with no locks, belts, or brakes.
The whole damn carnival to myself.
Scrubbing the floor in my underwear.
A.M. radio crackling over and over and over.
The church supper.
The unwashed dishes.
The pots and pans.
Sorbet at midnight.
The buy-one-get-one-free life.
The sorrowful mysteries.
The gun at my head.
The twelve apostles.
The wind in the trees like breathing.
Pentecost, swimming before dawn.
The heart, the heart, the heart.

Two Companions in the ICU

One step down,
two bruised trees besieged
by water. Beasts swimming
easily in the rough discolored spots.
Sometimes brain fades: red, mauve.
Squinting, two random silhouettes shrouded
against sky.
I cannot interpret this feverish chemical circus.
Am I asking for a handout, a hand-up,
breath work harnessed, an afterthought, an invader,
an adoration, organically speaking. Unruffled, puffs
of fluid sluice effortlessly through
me, silently infusing, engulf
a mere protoplasm, grounded by neurons,
each inspiration confined,
spiraling down into greenish drifts
cast like nets. Or roads on maps, spines curling, leading nowhere.
My flight path continues, coasts,
remote, unerring. Out of the breezeless
boggy fog steps a medium into a clearing.
She is neither grave nor irritable.
She is a cinema playing a rusty accordion
that only makes a wheezing drone and scrape
as it labors in and out. I'm on
tenet hooks, pedestrian, disposable. I need her splendor,
plead her to tell me how this will
all come out. Silent, she smiles, a torch burning
for hundreds of years, angelic,
touch slightly opaque, delineating
in first light. No air purifiers,
she barters for me, calm, windless.
I am airborne. I succumb,
beckon this remote resurrection, draw breath,
confined, a blue blossom rooted in my chest.

Life is but...

I prefer floating down the Niobrara slowly
Life employs a dream, lush
and humid, thick as sweat.
Floating like a blue-black cloud
in a wet sky, floating like puffs
of smoke
exhaled after holding
too long, floating like a hot air balloon
in the perfect blue sky. Floating like miles
and miles of green grass, just waiting
to be rolled in, floating like a kid
floating alone for the first time.
I am startled by the congregation of cranes,
the whole church of them, singing Alleluia
as they dance in the spirit. There is no predicting
the turn of the bend,
where one will beach on a sandbar,
the current speeding up, out of control.
Capsize, dump the life raft, suffer blue skin.
feel the way carefully in the present
moment, but sway and sway,
not even a remnant of a life preserver.

Not Exactly a Supermarket in California

If truth is beauty,
I am a liar, and he—
He is half my age, fussing
with the phone
the grumpy older
man gave him,
the one who keeps mumbling about
"the Government and the Corporate
world's method of keeping
tabs on us."
Now stop.
To ask him his age
would be more than slightly
creepy; but there's nothing wrong
with noticing beauty
wherever you go.
The kindest thing
you can do is be kind
because this is hell on
the revolving charge plan.
Even if the garish florescent
lights and crackly PA system
were taken out by executive order,
dismal remains. You can't scrub dismal
away. It gets under your nails
and tires and weakens you.
I admit to getting a little caught
up in admiring his elbow-
length chestnut hair,
and he had to ask me my phone number twice,
so the people on the
other end could find me.
From your mouth to God's ear, I whispered,

smiling encouragingly.
I used to work at this place
and it's 89 percent mean
customers. I recall no beef
with the managers.
O youthful phone man
with all the answers
(about electronics),
put that plastic bag away,
for I have only two items,
and they are both
going in my satchel grande.
He hands me my new, activated phone.
I'm blushing from the tip
of my toes to what my
best-selling friend Rebecca
calls "God's highlights."

Another Thing I Would Not Tell My Mother.

Me and the pastor's son—John—
drank grape Kool-aid
and vodka one summer
til we passed out on the riverbank.
A true friend, he held
my head while I regurgitated
in various shades of violet. Later, my hand.
He was angling, all right,
but I wasn't a fish
to be caught and he knew it.
We had been there since before sunset
picking out smooth stones,
tonguing names of small towns:
Nodaway, Clarinda, Nishnabotna -
The cottonwood
sent the breeze through
us like magic. Our faces painted
with excitement, we shed
our clothes and danced
like hooligans before jumping
in, sliding under the cool
water of time. In the distance
a dog barked, regular with rhythm.
It's that old dog of dawn
that reminds us why we do
everything, stripping down
in front of Time
to reveal who we really are.

The View From Here

Poets are always going on about the moon

-Todd Baker

Every time I stop what I'm doing,
notice the full moon, glaring, glowering.
Her perfectly round face and her
smooth skin stop me cold.
I am taken by her bold beauty,
iridescent, pearl-glow over the landform,
writing the way with her cold true light.

I am also astounded,
when a plane flies over head,
silently ripping the envelope
of sky like a clearinghouse sweepstakes letter.

You have won the sweepstakes. You are lovely and breathing.
You are here and now, drinking a cup of coffee, a beer, a smoothie.
It matters not what time it is,
for the plane travels through four time zones
to get to its destination.
Clocks are man-made. Time is not.
What I mean to say is,
you cannot stop the stream of time.
It keeps flowing, filling.
You can only stand there,
helpless, laughing,
befuddled
as it washes over you,
as it slides away.
You need not lose your sense of wonder, noticing the plane,
notice something you never get tired of seeing blaze across the sky.

Have You Seen the Moon, Dave Barger?

When the wind blows, she tells secrets—
but she tells them in another language
so no one will know.
She grins at the dark sky, waits, inscrutable.
The sky knows how to keep secrets.
The moon pulls herself up by her
moon-straps, hands and arms.
She glows from the exertion. She looks smashing,
a pearl of great price.
For the sky to sing, she carefully
tests the tune on her pitch-pipe, low and solid.
She sings hymns, but no one can hear.
She sings blues like smoky jazz
in a back beat club,
a tattered type of club
far off the main drag.
All the jazz players here
are at least one hundred years old.
There are five centuries
of musical expertise in this joint.
The joint reeks of weed. No one cares.
They nod their heads in time to the beat,
eyes half shut, they sway in time,
snap the syncopation,
roll and yell. They howl.
The wolf's at the door,
they all know that,
but no one seems to care.
Laid bare, they hang cool
waiting for the next note,
the one that floats out the window
into the star-filled sky.
The stars, punctures in the sky,

let in the light.
The moon smiles, amused,
opens her mouth and says,
  "Shoop a doop be boop oooooh yeah!"

At the star-watching party

I.
The sky unrolls from the earth,
an endless black carpet.
The earth rolls by in slow motion
like a curve ball.
We lie on a concrete slab—
stars cascade down like a blizaard.
The natives, slightly amused
at the wild-eyed wonder
of city folks.
We are smaller than we thought, our journey
to light simple but arduous

II.
Lewis and Clark used to measure
time by distance
and I never quite got that
but I'm beginning to see that
as we rocket and ricochet
through this wind tunnel of night
time and distance dissipate
with equal furiousity
as the wild, uncompromising
river would.

III.
Time and all of its principalities
may come to an end
but what about these two teenagers
and this middle-aged woman
breathing in and out gratefully
sailing gracefully in a cardboard box
in a riverless river?
Beneath us the earth spins—
Your eyes, old as forests.
I hand you a piece of the moon,
quartered like a pear.

Christmas Eve at deLeon's Mexican Restaurant

I've never mentioned
the crinkles around her eyes
when she smiles
as we dine on supper of beans
and beef and guacamole,
chopped tomatoes and cilantro
and two kinds of sauce, red and green.
How beautiful the fiber optic tree glowing
in the center of the restaurant!
The tired and beautiful young couple,
the man and his very pregnant,
all of nineteen, wife.
How beautiful the spotted
Christmas cows
lowing soft so as not to wake the Christ Child
Everything else is closed
and we are snowed in. The place is packed with anticipation.
A wedding was cancelled
due to inclement weather
and there's all this Mexican wedding cake
that needs to be eaten.
Suddenly three sets of
disco lights flashing red and white
fly by. No one looks up.
Everyone is busy eating and talking.
"Must be the three wise guys," she notes.
I crack a smile.
Right this minute,
everything is perfect—
pine incense, refried beans.
The door opens. More weary, hungry
pilgrims struggle in.
I hear chimes, a choir of angels.

For Dana, on her 19th birthday

Dear Dana,

When you were born,
your wail rocked the cosmos.
The moon began by asking

for your skin-care regime while
the sun, unused to competition,
retreated, pouting.

Your laugh is sparkling champagne.
(Both your mother and I
hope you don't drink too much.)

Also, honeybees wish they were you,
dancing dizzily into the sun. I should tell
you heights are nothing to you,

since you began your life
marching right up to the edge
of the precipice and shouting
to hear your voice echo back to you.

You know how when you sing
and a single syllable
slides into the next note?
Just so, the seconds and hours

converge,
sunflower clocks turning slowly
in the sun, a breath. You are rooted

in the thistle of my love.
I would give you a stone, something
solid, dear vineyard, dear sunflower.

Why Love is Like Bipolar Disorder, Only Not As Fun

For my niece.

Because you have a snarky plexiglass shield
and yet you are speechless
and your eyes are blue like oceans people only dream of
and you cannot help yourself to text him at 3 a.m.
    hoping for a glimpse of the light he took back too quickly.
Because you were a fool for believing
and because you died and he resurrected you
and because you are in love with your life.
Because you will never love again.
Because you have crushes on internet boys with names like
    Studboy and Big One
Because he will take you where you never imagined
and set you quietly sobbing back on earth.
Because he tastes like raspberry and looks like an angel – a fallen angel.
And he will love you for your body,
but end up loving your mind too
and you will cherish him
and you will feel like tearing him limb from limb
and you will want to die quickly and painlessly.
Because you are a container for quivers.
Because you will lose all your senses.
It will be like falling down a deep well
blindfolded, arms tied behind your back.
Because analogies suck,
and smart ass can only carry you so far
and no one will be able to talk you out of it
and you are both a giver and a plunderer
and you will mean yes and say no.
Because he is white knuckles, the roller coaster with no locks and no brakes.
And each cracked heart spiders out into infinity.
And you are calling his name long after he is gone.
Because even his name on your tongue,
dribbling like saliva to your shoulders, your breasts, your stomach,
even his name sounds like a sigh.

Crossing the Channel

We are crossing the same
English Channel
at different starting places.

He's outfitted with
a rubber
wetsuit
to stay warm and comfortable.

I've got this old swimsuit
about two sizes too large:
It floats like the sails
of a wrecked ship adrift
woefully bereft of supplies and resources.

He's buffing his nails
with the brains of old girlfriends.

Blue skies, he says, cracking open that
break-your-heart smile.
He squints, amused,
lights a cigar, puffs,
waits patiently for the opening bell.

I'm not sure how
I should put these pieces together
if it's even the same puzzle
we're looking at.

I exhale. Strictly by the rules, I tell him.
No cheating.

Is it cheating if no one saw? he says, grinning even wider.
I shiver, staring at what must be the shoreline, somewhere.
Gasping for breath while he sails
by, cocksure, with his fully-furnished coxswain.
If only I could see through the fog.

Tai Chi Under the Elms

"Moving slowly through heavy air as if in a dream,"
my instructor intones, face calm, unreadable.
I'm having trouble staying in the moment,
this area of hypotheses where everything comes together.
My instructor smells of sandalwood.
Where he moves, sandalwood wafts out.
Where his hipbone juts out of his pants,
a tattoo of Kells, carefully braided. I'm fighting being here,
my thoughts running into rivers,
splitting into rivulets,
and pooling further down my thought streams.
Dogpaddling in the stream of consciousness.
Sensei demonstrates the next move:
"The Golden Wheel of Life." I think he made this up, but,
obediently I follow, a small leaf
quivering in the wind, blown about as I will.
My arms move backwards as they should.
Wait—I have no arms. I am the universe.
One small step, me, sun, wind, leaves,
softly dappling shadows.
I am buzzed with delight, mixing the air thoroughly,
now praying smoke filled prayers
for the poor souls who never learned to pour themselves
out into the ocean of this moment.
I am breathing,
my breath is a prayer
my breath is food and drink
or is the air my food and drink?
I am carving designs in air,
describing figure eights of eternity,
egg, heart, sunburst,
arcs of joy, Fibonacci shells.
I am a green tree planted in midwestern soil.
I am a bird floating on warm thermals,
I am waking to the dream that is my life.

The Girl's Guide to Hunting and Fishing
(Part of the Wal-Mart series)

At 8:12 p.m. he swept, unkempt, camo-clad, casual, rumpled, through my lane. Ground beef, chips, granola bars, cookies, and Jack Daniels. When I asked him how he was, he replied, "Better than most. I'm not six feet under after all." He had a nice smile, and his eyes were a summer sky before the storm. Though I've never done it, all of a sudden I wanted to go hunting and fishing in the worst way. I logged out, threw my apron down, and followed him to his '59 Bel Air all the way to sunrise.

The Road Least Traveled

is the one at the junction of County 20
Highway 71, Highway 175,
and Interstate 39.
These innocent spatters
clattering on my windshield
have turned to snow.
Snow, and I am a voice crying in the wilderness,
"Twenty to 29, 39 to 30, or 30 to 59 to Interstate 80?"
All roads lead home, eventually,
the snow followed me
insidiously
and semis
picked fights with me,
riding my tail
all the way to Denison. (I tried
not to think about sliding
into the ditch. But I refuse
to budge for truckers. Those fuckers
can find their own way. "Anyone
that far up my ass better be pulling my hair,"
my bestie says.) Oh Denison.
Denison, Iowa—home of Donna Reed
and her Performing Arts Center.
You have to love small towns.
They try so hard, and often succeed with me.
Apparently Donna's sunshine
melted the snow. True story, because
it was clear all the way down 30
past Dow City, where my friends
the Bahrs are buried on a big hill
with a heart stopping view;
past Dunlap, which just looks worthy
of another visit with its old-fashioned

town square;
past Woodbine's
annual Apple Festival,
and the crown jewel,
the Museum of Religious Arts
between Logan and Missouri Valley.
You should go, if only to view a box
of nun dolls under glass.
Highway 30, where me and a train paced
each other all the way
to Missouri Valley,

his side markings flashing
off the occasional light,
looking for all the world
like windows to spring.

Malvern, Iowa

sounds like a stern woman
with a honey-colored beehive.

The community building was solid
brick, music on two levels,
a formal stage downstairs and a circle jam
upstairs, where mandolins and banjos accompanied
a four-year-old girl singing "You are my sunshine"
off-key. The room doubled for a gymnasium
and a theater. The downstairs was lit
with flickering florescent, the wallpaper
peeling, coffee and ice tea were set out
in urns, paper cups nearby. The fashion statement was
cowboy hats and those other hats advertising seeds.
A couple stared
as I began taking pictures, but they paid no mind
to the two elderly ladies waltzing with
each other. The band sang songs
about jail and Jesus and Mama and Missin' You.

All around me the night was filled
with moist scent
stars gathering about me
as I slid over each hill
toward the bright lights
on the horizon.

The Cherry Picker

The old man in the cherry picker smokes,
strings white lights with care
and ease, knowing
he will light up the whole world
with his lights. He wears
a dirty woolen cap. The wind says, *Hush*.
The traffic lights change. There is no traffic
in his small cage. There is no audience
cheering him on, just the sharp branches
cackling softly, creaking in protest
as he parts their legs,
bombed out of his mind.

A Cure for Pain

Would it seem a scrilege
to waste this time on tears:
given all prisms, even the muddy Mo,
resembles onyx tonight. So
turn. The river you step in now
is not the water you stood in
yesterday. Step away and pirouette
through soft hushed snow
into gleaming night.

Because all the rest is a leap of faith

Even when Death sends you memos
in the form of your beating heart
you can ignore it.

I hold you firm, away
from treacherous gravity.

Your feet: strawberry plants, pressing into the earth.

You step back, amused,
I hand you the lens.
We are smaller than we thought.

Acknowledgments

"After Larry Levis' Motel Room"   *The New*

"At the Calmar Guesthouse"   *Hiram Poetry Review*

"Momento Mori"   *Filling the Empty Room*

"At the Star-Watching Party"   *Midwest Quarterly*

"The Carrying Over,"   *ArLiJo/Gival*
"Days Lost," "First hey walk in your feet"

"Cemetery"   *Blast Furnace*

"My Relationship with God," "At the Downtown Y,"   *The Flatwater Stirs*
"Death on the Installment Plan"

"Another Thing I Would Not Tell My Mother"   *Misbehaving Nebraskans*

"A Cure for the Pain"   *Ardent*

ABOUT THE AUTHOR

Author photo credit: Al Viola

HEIDI HERMANSON has been published in *Midwest Quarterly, Hiram Poetry Review, PlainSpoke, the Omaha World Herald* ("Nebraska On A Dollar a Day") and elsewhere. She co-edited the award-winning *The Untidy Season: An Anthology of Nebraska Women Poets* (Backwaters Press), and organized the first Poets' Chautauqua at the State Fair. Heidi has directed four ekphrastic shows which she describes as a marriage between visual art and poetry. From 2006 to 2012 she ran "Naked Words", a monthly open mike. In 2008 Heidi received her MFA from the University of Nebraska at Omaha, where she studied with South Dakota poet Laureate Lee Ann Roripaugh. In 2010, she won the Omaha Public Library's annual poetry contest and performed her winning work accompanied by Silver Roots, a New York-based violin and flute duo. In 2014, Heidi became a nominee for the Pushcart Prize.She has read at the John R Milton Conference in Vermillion, SD, at the Bowery Poetry Club in New York City, at Tunes in the Town Square (which features poetry at the band's break) in Ralston, Nebraska, on the Kerry Pedestrian Bridge over the Missouri, and at the Roebuck Pub in London. In her spare time, she hopes to open a library of maps to towns that no longer exist and learn the dialects of the seventeen-year cicada.

CPSIA information can be obtained
at www.ICGtesting.com
Printed in the USA
LVHW091735100319
610121LV00001B/105/P

9 781622 882137